DRIFTOLOGY

DRIFTOLOGY

⁎

DEBORAH BERNHARDT

NEW MICHIGAN PRESS
TUCSON, ARIZONA

NEW MICHIGAN PRESS
DEPT OF ENGLISH, P. O. BOX 210067
UNIVERSITY OF ARIZONA
TUCSON, AZ 85721-0067

<http://newmichiganpress.com/nmp>

Orders and queries to nmp@thediagram.com.

Copyright © 2013 by Deborah Bernhardt.
All rights reserved.

ISBN 978-1-934832-40-0. FIRST PRINTING.

Printed in the United States of America.

Design by Ander Monson.

Cover art: Letha Kelsey, *Sun as Horn,* 2006, acrylic, watercolor, pastel, conté, wax, oil, and plaster on panel. Courtesy of the artist (lethakelsey.com).

CONTENTS

Driftology *[Episode One]*   1
Driftology *[Episode Two]*   2
Driftology *[Episode Three]*   4
Driftology *[Episode Four]*   5
Driftology *[Episode Five]*   6
Driftology *[Episode Six]*   7
After Stuff Smith and/or Steve Reich   8
Formality   10
Letterboxed   12
Bernoulli   14
The Beginning of Open Movement   17
Industrial Photos   20
Helium   21
Roving Frame for Silk and Möbius Shanty   23
Aktionspreise   27

Notes   31
Acknowledgments   33

for my parents

✲✲

…a continuous present a beginning again and again and again and again, it was a series it was a list it was a similarity and everything different it was a distribution and an equilibration.

—Gertrude Stein, "Composition as Explanation"

DRIFTOLOGY [EPISODE ONE]

Let not one put asunder any content.

Aggregator articles stitched
in the manner articulators

make of bones one flesh, flush and complete,
yet distinct, bric-a-brac intact,
                                      a Melvillean marriage—

extremes of one. Each bone in its floating trap, Sugar Snap.
The remainder of my dearly is a tingling artifact, saturated red.

One undiluted cell which I weigh
in a nanomolecular cantilever's

microchannel.
                    Blue vessels scatter dear light yet out of skin,

blue is Rayleigh scattered, flashing

in a TV series rerun, non-diegetic light

in a character's eye, a heterochromia

Lynchian pin. Oh kitschy catch light,

sideways, specular, keeping eyes alive,

even those of my transistor in drift.

DRIFTOLOGY [EPISODE TWO]

Continuity errors
in the body's motion picture.
Despite the cutting, cutting floor,

or due to it: when splicing
the continuous, thus creating
continuity, we punctuate equilibrium,

too rapidly creating variation.
The butterfly effect, if and when
the butterflies are giants.

Little of long red lengths
are affected by air,
but perturbation of wings

causes *meet* to be *moat* and *oh* to be *you*.
The Great Vowel Shift,
if vowels find coordinates on chaotic,

unsolvable waves. *Swing Amplification of Shear Alfvén Waves through Periodical Density Variations in a Conductive Medium*. Area Author Has No Idea Either. Vowels shift Romantically, romance

splitting their seams, whaling
through blood-brain barrier reefs
and spliced bone. We surf a channel,

and it leads to *a dispersed congregation
of our debris from civilization.* 7,200 packs
of spilled plastic floatees—

turtles, frogs, beavers, and ducks—
a Regatta of Venetian color—
gyrate around the jutting world.

The bathtub-intended whoopsadaisy vortices
will photodegrade, turning into nurdles, jots corrupting
the high seas. Artifacts occurring due to poor image registration

and corny vignetting. The thinner the layer,
the finer the luster! My *drishti* turns to sea,
and my achromat to the antimetabole.

Oh, satellite signal,
which barely departs,
and never reaches zero!

DRIFTOLOGY [EPISODE THREE]

Oh, lately my departed is a TV series rerun.

In HD Imagist resolution.
Lips blued-out like Laura Palmer's
when she was big time debris,

wasted to shore in a plastic drop cloth, bound
for the twice-Texas of the North Pacific Gyre

with her eyes blued-shut and lashed down.
Pretty as ice. Local Theme Music Contains
Key Shift. Badalamenti, Composer, Scales
Peaks; Has Been to Minor, and Back.

Violence all the more cartooned in this
sweet resolution, but narrative blood
is a channel programmed on a remote,

red gone primary in cycles. One season,
Twin Peaks' blood, the next, Sopranos' blood,
our cautery of spurts, our Land's End of incarnadine.
Grief Revival: Formal Feeling, or Boring Episode?

Mind your head, thoughts, you seashore junkyard.
I walked the walk to ungreet the one who walked here to mourn
with all America behind her. Local Woman Tamps Down Tone.

DRIFTOLOGY [EPISODE FOUR]

A slick ride, a riding on slicks,
a continent, the undiscovered country's

wild, wild seams. No inverted pyramid-style here.
Enhanced coupling enlightens one caliper of news

in a scrolling treadmill: Shoes Thrown at American Dog |
Double Dare Naughty Monkey Pumps, Auctioned.

In our wide age, my old age, peripheral vision stays put,
a steadfast dynasty of wideness. Wiggling on my right,

wiggling on my left, and a windshieldfull
of frontal foci. When I look at a banquet-wide photo,

I know how to enter: at each measure. Grab the shadow
and the shadow's cousin. Slant through unburned light

and velutinous paths. But an imprinted beach is a wider challenge—
I know not where to think—I get to the palm of Stevens

and my mind is feathers, and then my mind is strewn, and then collected,
and once it is, the particular pleasure is the dodging tool atop, bloodletting

a funnel of light, waving me
lighter than myself.

DRIFTOLOGY [EPISODE FIVE]

Bobbing sing-along style—
atop waveforms, atop lit up words
in the De Forest Phonofilm
that sees the lit up words in you—

a cheery beached buoy named Number 5
shines simply, cuts a Great Figure,

as gold figure 5's do.
It is a wild, rank place,
and there is no flattery in it.
Studying the decaying fields

of old satellite waves beaming old TV,
a forensic team of bad actors

does a far reading of *Superradiance*
by Nonlocal Wave Coupling
of Light and Excitons
in CuCl Thin Films. Charged

with Attempted Tonal Shift.
Despite continental divide and drift,

shift is one part if,
two parts speech. The verb "shift"
calibrates the noun "shift,"
gearing us up for coasting continuity.

DRIFTOLOGY [EPISODE SIX]

"Next-Door Neighbors": Wasilla Visible from Pacific Trash Vortex.

Local Library Circulates Currents of Universal Being.

Thoreau Encounters *Wide-Open and Staring Eyes*

Yet Lustreless, Dead-Lights; or Like the Cabin Windows

of a Stranded Vessel, Filled with Sand. Thirty seconds of blue
flare in Luminol, a forced bloom of hemoglobin
on the brain's floor. Purpling halo of prose.
Invisible seam of departing blood unseen
yet nay, it is; I know not "seems."
Backstory on the DVD package
says it is like parking in Italy:
making a space that is not there.
Like making the green one red.

AFTER STUFF SMITH AND/OR STEVE REICH

his name followed by a cut
his name followed by a cut
his name followed by a cut
I did not watch

use your whole arm
when you bow
slices of air

détaché
tuning your radius

pressing the sound
arm against
a sea stage left

by sinew to the moment
commissioned choral
Daniel Pearl Variations
layers of regress

and at the catachresis
of third remove
my tinny harp

too sharp
no no
climb up that stair

household instrument on
Kármán Vortex Street
unsteady separation

of viscous over a body
singing of
suspended lines

telephone or power
Oh-spel-dah-doo-di

he says in the video
there is a street named after
my great-grandfather
Chaim Pearl

his name followed by a cut
his name followed by a cut
his name followed by a cut
I did not watch

FORMALITY

On me like sprayed stars,
blast in the atelier,
splayed below the acrylic horizon

of soldiers running past the fold
of a magazine—
not a chamber, or the storehouse of the arrow,

but digital modernity upon a creased war
which, in fact, is over, we want. It is said: *the error already begins
when someone is about to buy a stretcher and canvas.*

Mission Accomplished for these sailors who are on this ship on their mission,
or the error already begins when someone is about to say *crusade*.
You and I are the lower third, and as we close-caption,

I say again what I thought to be done saying,
oh my sloppiness. When I try to forget you,
one side of my brain sleeps. My breath is held as I would hold.

Would hold. You offer only
brief. A whale thinks not of breath held but breath taking,
and its breath taking sleep is hemisphere by hemisphere.

When the left side sleeps, the right navigates breath,
and while the right sleeps, the left oversees breath.
The left of the human senate, with a mere skeleton,

prevented recess appointments, holding pro forma sessions,
neither chamber adjourning. The whale's never-recess
is chamber by chamber. The whale flips up a tail

which looks to be the biggest butterfly,
Darstellung fluttering deep. Representative one,
you misplace my consent and semaphoring

along my legislative body. I hope
for more than two-thirds.
I speak, as long as necessary, on this issue.

LETTERBOXED

[T]he figures move   And so it was   widescreened
not a gray sky   *but a world*   and telecined   This
is my stunt double   If I were double,   I'd file
online,   refund faster   Security might stop me
How will you know   if I end this by choice   If I
had extra choices   I'd be a long-haired star, I'd be

a harlot star, Queen of Sheba, he bop, Ba-Re-Bop
Tender death   *but a world*   Can-do safe harbor
for the acting governor's sleep   *the figures move*
Reenactment   on the History Channel: are we
sufficiently enlightened?   If not,   pay $25 extra
Suitcase full of letters   Lifting-Line Theory:

real-world wings   in a video slot   So open and close
The sky is tender   I left   a lap of stone   Not one flower
open and shut   *not a gray sky*   Look   under the matte
framing action   Culture jam   *figures move*   a Whirl-mart
Glittery carts   The moment you recognize   non-buyers
file behind them   Crashing   tortuosity by induction

into a portrait   We clank our spoons   We scrape our chairs
too many decibels: conserve   Sprawling on lapis,   lazy,
eating tapas   Hibernating bats   slip from an upstairs
Warming wakes them   Hand-feed till spring   *It is not
a gray sky, but a world in mourning*   Bless the restoration
of the aspect ratio   *in which the figures move*   span to chord.

BERNOULLI

How long do you wait
in the station?—

| on the double page |
of day and paper | .

Original lines debriefed,
flighted.

Where are your own lungs?—
I wanted to ask,

some hours removed,
in a crazy.

System restore.
Withstand clear.

The feeling is painting.
To know you better.

Wherever I am walking,
severed trees

are light-shine clean. Rust
Oleum can, rusted. Carpet moss-covered.

We had your bivouac
all set. You were expected

for a retake of your page. Familiars
"like" my little of little. We cannot, do not,

post your *lickspoon darkling*—
even in this botch of body.

We do not post your titular
morticians, your titular coroners,

though they—severally—
O proffering nips.

Too punctual dartcoiner.
Littlest of us,

birds, overlook bits
of the littlest still,

red berries, some red not nipped,
no need for debridement.

Light of a clearing,
valour and act—

air—plume—here—
ventilator, your own breaths,

and the fire that thee then.
Too-too-too not where.

Tout whirring you hier.
Taupe plage widestnabulation.

Tout all leverage two spins.
Wear elegant stays for the vessel.

Words, your vassals, so va-va-va-not,
sail-not. Knot-wood knocks stay.

Yes would knock whose their? Yours.
Stasis budding in vases,

sifting for a banter. Remember
that time

that that that stamped?
Faster over the top,

air creating a region
of low pressure, thus lift.

THE BEGINNING OF OPEN MOVEMENT

> *The idea was to make a ground of ropes with clothes threaded through them… It was called "Floor of the Forest"!… I was always accumulating gestures, then going back to the beginning.*
> —Trisha Brown

Paradox maritime leaves flip plus flash. Bright-pale underside. Pretending to be whale tails. If beech trees can pretend, then convicts may.

Peristaltic waves of barbed wire equal sea. Silver periphery. Cinder blocks equal distant sandbars. Photons faux-splitting.

Sauntering in the square equals floor of the forest. See the crisscross of the beige. Grainy at the beginning of open movement.

Legible at the beginning of open movement. Commissary shoes and shades. With, to be precise, some white t-shirts, some gray.

Looks like any street's college if we squint. At the beginning of open movement for all housing units, I wait. Sorting my flimsy Socratic props which are not of the not-bound-by-language.

The War on Windows keeps inmates opaquely milk-glassed. Joe the Bureau of Prisons would like to stop eyes. The world space grove is guarded.

Sealed by paint as leaden as some footsteps. Neatly clicking processes do skip or buzz at a sill-framed vista. An ecstasy of trees reroutes television beams and their tidy satellites.

The schoolmarmish mantra, stop looking out the window, is wardenish here. Musing graphed over undulant green cannot be tracked or cleanly sealed. Waveforms across the quad.

A good surfer becomes part of a wave. A good choreographer lets waves become a part. Gestures tousling gestures. Dangling dancers. Flocking garments equal fronds.

Space revolving under erasure, residing alongside itself. One quanta away from "Floor of the Forest" is the dance of the marigold quad.

Lilliputian stinkflowers, quality trees, and a bench for transparency. For sitting away from cellies and other ear hustlers. Housing units blare. Guarding is a noisy style.

Adrenalin-coated-jangle of numbly draping metal. A good prison guard has a mindset of *I am not them*. Cool octopi keys decorating the work pants.

A person from the street wears a red-button body alarm. Unnecessary, that. If one wave threatened, the others would straighten it out.

The beginning of open movement. All housing units. My students, like social birds or brides, process. Spooky action at a distance.

Original definition decayed. Telling the difference. Being-thus. Between quoted and not. Blood in a wine barrel and the wine as well.

That they were at the beach. Peristaltic waves of barbed wire equal sea. Splitting light. Are you in the car with that?

INDUSTRIAL PHOTOS

Texture is composed peaks arose. Outside itself
turns, whips, and peels. A fine toxic dust
tamps down the want to touch. No, it amps. The
be and the am fall down, hardhats in progression
à la Magritte. Down, down. Be amber.

Churn eight bungalows
with all their subtle nails and timber
the little metal of them, all their True Value,
in the "Will it Blend" blender—then you'll get
the warehoused texture you crave.

Text her. Or are you made of w(o)o(u)(l)d (a)
(coulda) (shoulda). All her dust ire
falls in rue him. Rust and wood appeal
in their oxy-hewn, tamarind hue,
their selfsame oxytones. Beaminess.

Give saturation minutes to beams
'round beams. Saltatorial light says salutations. Beamfill!
Light tailors to shape, pitches woo to the beamsome
beam in the eye, to texture. Be a thrice: soothe, ruffle,
develop. All hope, you who enter here.

HELIUM

Beloved, who nearly never repulses,
causes Bremsstrahlung—
the free-free radiation
bricolaging

light and limb.
When Skype's pixels
consolidate, and my love in the field
has a Matrix mouth, iMind'sEye

our resolution. Without
seat assignment, I storyboard
the destination.
I don't perplex

epitaph and epigraph. I do
twine epithalamium and epithelium.
Prefix or prix fixe: already fastened

because the billionth more of matter than antimatter
is enough. It asymmetries matter into being.
Particles sharing the same rate of curl

are mirror charges, spinning opposite
but evenly. A pair of skewbacks,
as they are called,
are enough to support an arch.
An arch

is a brow between quips.
Under skew never tinny
and the reach of the arch,

unlike that of the Attic shape,
does touch. It is
the ace of hips.

ROVING FRAME FOR SILK AND MÖBIUS SHANTY

Early plank floors
are rarely tongue-and-grooved.

Keep the graining
relations bare—

unfinished antique
heart pine. Propinquant

to a post-industrial
blaze. Above

is an epic of scuffs.
Without Astaire, even,

yesteryear's floorboards
are shuttle-bobbined

as ceilings.
Silk reeling,

bodikins shush.
Floorboards

yearn. Even
pulsar scruff

epicycles above
building blaze,

dustily, sidereal
to quid pro piquant

yet pining hearts.
Antique

unfinished relations
to bare grain.

Groove andirons.
Tug anchors. Rarely

does Planck time
flourish so errantly.

When antiquity's thread-warp passes,
longing is so long, its intentions

weave a golden doubloon loom
and loft as linden and oak,

one trunk *(made) of a two-fold body.*
Clenching leaves,

queries eternally concentric.
Non-anxious care,

like Marc and Bella
floating over the Dvina, over

a geometric town. Fake wood paneling is
the anywither that raised me. Whorls,

though too regular, diveable.
Fickle bedtime arborist—

identified the whorls, blinked,
identified them again, traversed

their knock-off knots
many knots deep. Blankets

fashioned bed as boat,
confusion of sea and forest.

Ceiling fan rotor,
whirl adorable Möbius wings.

Infinity's baluster, unbolt
but to ponder a stop in the mind,

O run out. How
to build *some shanties of houses*,

some shanties of chapters & essays?
Ticking, undevil. Trundle, all under.

Words, do not
foreshorten,

unless that brings us syncopation—
tocking the doubloon bed.

Window glass, rest thyself.
Gingerly, as not to injure time.

Wave-particle,
fiddle double-slit silk strands

through the roving frame.

AKTIONSPREISE

Put on a fishing vest.
Now you are ready-
made-to-wear an event score.

Divvy your dictionary
to pockets in your vestment.
Pluck words you can loop

in a daisy chain, or save
to an ittybyte flash drive. Flash my Daisy,
or pull one. Give a free compliment

from your neighbor's Berlitz phrase book.
I'm so happy that you didn't sneeze.
Pull up the corners

of your mouth. Say bygones be bygones
to wrinkles. Foster such a tension. Double
your pleasure. Anchor our external direct action

with the power of economic withdrawal.
Witness the trellis of response
to the Memphis Sanitation Strike last speech.

If you are where I am thinking,
listen to « Le cygne » down the hall
and, simultaneously, a Benjamin Patterson video

about the Museum of the Subconscious.
Go to a station under the earth.
You will not see the landmark

when leaving the train, but just when
you arrive, you see you are right.
This is the end of the line,

so you cannot take a false direction.
Adjust your map for the intersection
of rhetorical and Bermuda.

Or, play the triangle.
It may sound like dinner time,
so take a bite. Sweep off your feet.

Rub, scrub, twist. Dissolve
the difference between bass and broom
and hawk and cello. If you have

a music stand, put all the rests
together. Go into a passage.
Then you are there

where you are expected.

NOTES

Donovan Hohn discusses driftology in his *Harper's* article "Moby-Duck" and his book *Moby-Duck*.

Stanza eight of "Driftology *[Episode Two]*" quotes Captain Charles Moore.

The passage in "Driftology *[Episode Six]*" from Henry David Thoreau's *Cape Cod* also appears [thank you, Joy Ladin] in Robert Lowell's "The Quaker Graveyard in Nantucket."

Italicized language in "Formality" is from Joseph Beuys and a White House press secretary.

Italicized language in "Letterboxed" is from a letter by Egon Schiele. "Whirl-mart" is a "participatory experiment" first enacted in 2001 at a branch of the facility whose name is similar to "Whirl-mart."

Two lines in "Bernoulli" are from Elizabeth Bishop's translation of "January First" by Octavio Paz. Italicized lines are by Morgan Lucas Schuldt. Coinages and Gerard Manley Hopkins misprisions are for Morgan Lucas Schuldt.

The last two stanzas of "The Beginning of Open Movement" use a line from "Snow for Wallace Stevens" by Terrance Hayes and a line from Leslie Scalapino's "aeolotropic series."

"Helium" is for Darren Jackson.

"Roving Frame For Silk and Möbius Shanty" quotes a June 29, 1851 letter from Herman Melville to Nathaniel Hawthorne.

"Aktionspreise" references Benjamin Patterson's analysis of audience participation during Dr. Martin Luther King, Jr.'s April 3, 1968 speech and other work from *Benjamin Patterson: Born in the State of FLUX/us* (Nassauischer Kunstverein Wiesbaden, 2012). Thank you, Benjamin Patterson.

ACKNOWLEDGMENTS

Grateful acknowledgment to the editors, readers, and staffs of publications in which these poems first appeared:

"Driftology [Episode One]," *Volt*.
"Driftology [Episode Two]," "Driftology [Episode Three]," and
 "Driftology [Episode Four]," *The Offending Adam*.
"Formality," *Tikkun*.
"Letterboxed," *Trickhouse*.
"Bernoulli," *TYPO*.
"The Beginning of Open Movement" and "Aktionspreise,"
 American Letters & Commentary.
"Industrial Photos," *Free Verse*.
"Helium," *New American Writing*.

Grateful thanks to the Fine Arts Work Center in Provincetown, Hessen-Wisconsin Exchange Program, Hessischer Literaturrat, Literaturhaus Villa Clementine, Mo's Place in Shelburne Falls, Summer Literary Seminars, and Virginia Center for the Creative Arts for fellowships and residencies that made possible the completion of these poems.

Thank you, and a debt of love to Amy Avila, Taylor Baldwin, Lea Banks, Julian Billups, Charlie Conley, Ulrike Eisenträger, Maggie Golston, Jennifer Rosen Heinz, Hartmut Holzapfel, Darren Jackson, Janet Jensen, Lois Jensen, Kristi Maxwell, Boyer Rickel, Morgan Lucas Schuldt, Peter Trachtenberg, and Julia Wolf for company, factoid guidance, and revision guidance during the writing of these poems.

Thank you and a debt of love to Letha Kelsey for *Sun as Horn.*

Utmost gratitude to Ander Monson and New Michigan Press for what they do.

⁂

COLOPHON

Text is set in a digital version of Jenson, designed by Robert Slimbach in 1996, and based on the work of punchcutter, printer, and publisher Nicolas Jenson.

The titles are also in Jenson.

DEBORAH BERNHARDT is the author of *Echolalia* (Four Way Books, 2006).

⁂

NEW MICHIGAN PRESS, based in Tucson, Arizona, prints poetry and prose chapbooks, especially work that transcends traditional genre. Together with DIAGRAM, NMP sponsors a yearly chapbook competition.

DIAGRAM, a journal of text, art, and schematic, is published bimonthly at THEDIAGRAM.COM. Periodic print anthologies are available from the New Michigan Press at NEWMICHIGANPRESS.COM/NMP.

www.ingramcontent.com/pod-product-compliance
Lightning Source LLC
Chambersburg PA
CBHW031506040426
42444CB00007B/1226